The PS Factor

THE KEY TO PEAK MENTAL PERFORMANCE FOR LIFE

Dr. Thomas Crook III, Ph.D.

"A man's memory is
all that stands between
him and chaos."

A.L. Korsakoff

"A woman's memory is
all that stands between
a man and chaos."

Roland Gahler

This book is dedicated to those who
understand that the true fountain of youth
comes through a healthy mind and spirit,
not just a healthy body.

TABLE OF CONTENTS

" 'Wow!' the driver said, as I filled in the names of distant relatives he and his wife were trying to recall as they discussed the family reunion they had kindly invited me to attend. Eventually, he turned to me, raised his eyebrows and said, 'You're good!'

That I could remember all those names surprised even me (I am well known for forgetting names, rather than remembering them), but that sort of thing had been happening more and more often over the past few weeks. I sensed that my thinking was more acute and I felt mentally as sharp as in my early years.

Upon reflection, I realized the only different factor in my life was phosphatidylserine. I had been taking it for a couple of months now; my normally health-conscious lifestyle had not in any other way varied. That had to be it! I am convinced that phosphatidylserine has made the difference in my cognitive abilities and performance. I am resolved to make it a part of my normal health regimen." - Myra M.

INTRODUCTION

Donna so frequently locked her keys in her car that the local automobile association knew her by name.

Evelyn had an excellent vocabulary, yet frequently found herself groping for words, especially when she was a bit nervous. Soon she kept quiet in social situations, hoping no one would notice her awkwardness.

Sooner or later it happens. We forget the name of someone we just met, we grope for a word that's on the tip of our tongue, and we start to misplace keys and glasses. We put it down to being overworked or distracted, but inside we secretly wonder if we're losing it. Quite frightening, really. Some of us may even start to avoid situations that require basic skills, such as remembering names and faces.

The bad news is that trouble with memory and learning is a natural consequence of getting older.

Neuroscientists have names for this phenomenon: Age-Related Cognitive Decline (ARCD) or Age Associated Memory Impairment (AAMI). Whatever term we use, the fact that we can't learn or remember as well as we used to, just because we're getting older, is very disconcerting.

What's the good news then? People need to realize that it is perfectly normal for certain memory abilities to decline with age and that these changes are not generally predictive of a serious problem. People with Age-Related Cognitive Decline may experience problems when a large amount of information must be learned quickly, particularly if it is abstract or unfamiliar information, and must be learned and/or recalled in the presence of other distracting stimuli.

Unless you're a fighter pilot or have another job where you must deal very quickly with massive amounts of incoming data, the kinds of memory abilities that decline can be strengthened through steps discussed in the following pages.

Another very important piece of good news is that the *highest* level of intellectual abilities does not decline as we get older. Take wisdom, for instance: The ideal age at which a human can learn to speak Chinese is probably five or six years old. However, the ideal age at which a human could effectively rule China might be in the seventh decade of life. While some cognitive functions decline with age, others improve. The news gets better.

Keep in mind, when you find you can't remember names, you have to read things more than once, or you're just a bit slower at learning new information, that these problems do not mean Alzheimer's Disease is looming. As tragic as it is, Alzheimer's Disease is rare and happens to very few people until quite late in life. For example, between the ages of 65 and 75, fewer than 2% of the population will develop Alzheimer's Disease or another dementing disorder.

"The good news is that the most important intellectual functions do not decline with age...The abilities to synthesize, analyze and reach a conclusion get better."

Dr. Thomas Crook,
The Arizona Republic.

Just as we can take preventive measures to avoid heart disease by watching our fat intake, exercising regularly, and periodically having our blood pressure and cholesterol checked, we also can intervene and take preventive measures to conserve our cognitive functions, before they decline.

This book is written on the premise that you *can* offset the effects of age on the brain. Suppose a doctor handed you a prescription and said, 'take this and even though you're 65 years old, you'll be like 25 when you're finished.' We'd all take it. No one can promise you that for your body. However, with the brain we can say that. There is no reason why a 65-year-old can't function better than the average 25-year-old if he/she follows the simple strategies outlined in this booklet. In fact, a 65-year-old who has trained his brain to remember will be sharper than an untrained 25-year-old. Now, while that isn't true of everyone, it is true for most of us.

There are a number of ways to delay cognitive decline. The most important is taking a nutrient called phosphatidylserine, or PS. Although not a magic bullet, PS shows much promise in improving cognitive function, especially as we age. *More about PS later.*

CHAPTER 1

WHAT STAYS AND WHAT SLIPS AWAY?

"There are three things I always forget: names, faces, and...
I can't remember the other." Italo Svevo from the "Quote...Unquote"
Book of Love, Death and the Universe

It's somewhat heartening to know that other factors in our hectic lives can affect our ability to remember important facts – stress, disorganization, lack of concentration, just having more information to sort through as we age. Aside from these outside factors, Age-Related Cognitive Decline does happen to everyone eventually.

Several years ago we administered five computerized memory tests, measuring five different everyday memory abilities to approximately 4100 normal, healthy men and women. The research showed that by age 70 most of us still have our ability to remember a face; however, we've lost half the ability to remember someone's last name when given their first name.[i]

As you peruse the following tests, note the kinds of memory abilities that slip away.

TEST RESULTS: 18-year-olds to 70-year-olds

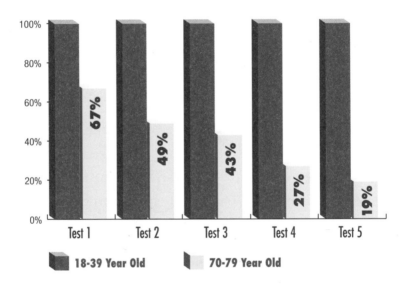

18-39 Year Old **70-79 Year Old**

The scores of 18-to 39-year-olds on five memory tests are set at 100%. Scores for the 70-to 79-year-olds are shown as a percentage of how well the 18-to 39-year-olds did.

TEST 1: Name that Face

On a computer screen you see 14 people, who appear one at a time and tell you their first names. The people appear again, but in a different order. When asked to name them, the average 18-to 39-year-old can remember five of the fourteen names. The average 70-to 79-year-old can remember fewer than two names.[ii]

TEST 2: First and Last Names

Six first and last names are shown on the computer screen. Then you're given each last name and asked for the corresponding first name. This procedure is repeated on two more occasions with the order of the names scrambled both times. Out of 18 chances to match first names with last names, the average 18-to 39-year-old is correct approximately 11 times, whereas the average 70-year-old is correct fewer than six times.[iii]

TEST 3: Telephone Number Recall

You're given a telephone number (with area code) to dial. After dialing the number from memory, you have to dial the number again because you're given a busy signal. The average 18-to 39-year-old can remember almost six of the 10 digits. The average 70-to 79-year-old can remember only about three digits.[iv]

TEST 4: The Grocery List

Fifteen items on a grocery list are shown one at a time on the computer screen and you are asked to recall the list from memory. The average 18-to 39-year-old can remember about 10 of the 15 items. The average 70-to 79-year-old can remember approximately seven items.[v]

TEST 5: Pick the New Face

A photo of a face appears on a computer screen. You touch the screen and the face disappears, and every eight seconds the faces are rearranged and a new face appears

"Scientists now know that as the brain gets older, some of its cells send out new "branches" – long, spidery projections called dendrites. These dendrites, which receive the chemicals necessary for information processing, can continue to grow longer and sprout new dendrites even in old age. Indeed, many experts speculate that dendritic branching may be responsible for what we call the 'wisdom of age.' The foundation of wisdom, of course, is the memory of life's experiences."

Bill Lawren, *New Choices Magazine*

until 25 faces are on the screen. The average 18-to 39-year-old can pick out the new face 21 out of 25 times. The average 70-year-old is successful 17 out of 25 times.[vi]

Age-related changes in brain function

The brain contains over 100 billion nerve cells, called neurons, which conduct electrical and chemical impulses. Over time the number of our neurons declines. While this might not pose a great problem, it can make a difference if the remaining neurons don't function as efficiently.

A thin membrane surrounds neurons, and from the membrane numerous filament-like protrusions extend. They look like the branches of a tree and are called 'dendrites' and they receive messages from other neurons and send them to the nucleus of the neuron. As we age, chemical and structural changes in the brain make the dendrites less effective at conducting and receiving impulses, so the electrical messages that help our cells generate memory and learn new things are not as lively as they are in a younger brain. Studies with animals show that the age-related loss of dendrites can be halted. Even better, research indicates that we can grow new dendrites just by challenging our brain with memory enhancement techniques.

- Levels of neurotransmitters, the chemical messengers in our brain, decrease with age.

- The hippocampus, a part of our brain that helps us learn new things and retain old information, loses a percentage of its cells each year.

- Chemical signals and electrical messages produced by our neurons jump across the synapses to other brain cells. To learn and make memories our neurons produce patterns of connections. If these patterns of connections are not used frequently they become less efficient in conducting electrical impulses and may even disappear altogether – little used memories disappear while frequently used memories remain. Brain scans show that older brains have fewer connections. A logical way to slow ARCD is to improve the conductivity of our neurons. This is where phosphatidylserine, or PS, can really help, as you'll see.

Some factors that compound age related changes

- Often, outside influences can interfere with our memories, dimming, confusing, rearranging, or even blocking them. These influences include perceptual problems we may develop with age such as reduced vision and hearing. While they do not directly interfere with memory, we have reduced control of what we want to remember.[vii]

- Prolonged stress has a negative affect on memory. All of us, young and old, experience stress during an average day. However, prolonged stress is harmful to the brain and can impair thinking ability even in the youngest and brightest. There is evidence that certain parts of the brain's memory system can actually atrophy (stop working) under assault by chronic sustained stress.

- Our lifestyle choices – alcohol, smoking, poor diet, lack of exercise, overall poor health – negatively affect our memory and learning. Just changing some of our habits can make a profound difference in our ability to learn and remember.

"Many things that occur when you grow old were just accepted – it just seemed natural that you'd end up on the front porch rocker. But with improvements in the diet, more exercise, drugs that prevent disease and now compounds like PS, normal developmental changes are no longer inevitable."

Dr. Thomas Crook
Prevention Magazine, August 1991.

CHAPTER 2

CAN WE HOLD BACK THE CLOCK? CAN OUR BRAINS STAY YOUNG AS WE GROW OLDER?

The answer is a resounding 'YES.' By incorporating certain nutrients, such as PS, into our diet, and changing our lifestyle to include exercise and good nutrition, we can help our brain retain its youthful vigor. Important, too, is paying attention to our stress levels, watching less television, and challenging our mind with creative and stimulating exercises.

The importance of memory screening tests

It's important for people to know how their cognitive abilities are affected by age. Dr. Parris Kidd comments on the importance of the tests that I designed with my team: "The Name-Face Recall and other tests of higher mental functions from Crook's group represent a new generation of common sense tests for higher mental functions. They give to Crook's findings an 'everyday' relevance that can be used by real people to get a real idea of how their higher mental functions are holding up against the passage of time."[viii]

Using sophisticated computerized techniques to simulate such tasks, researchers in fourteen countries have been able to measure the "normal" course of changes in learning and memory over the life span and also, how disease or trauma alter that course. They have also used the tests in the search for effective treatments for both 'normal' and disease-related changes in learning and memory.

How good are your memory skills? Take the test and find out.

It's easy to take the memory test in the privacy of your own home. Nobody's looking over your shoulder, watching you. While such a short test is not definitive, you will have a good idea of where you might want to improve. Or, perhaps you're one of the lucky few who score very high. Even so, the strategies suggested here will dramatically improve your memory and help you maintain optimal cognitive function for a lifetime. Either way, you can't lose.

"The tests we perform are not the usual tests. They relate to things we do in every day life such as remembering the names of people to whom we are introduced, recognizing people we have seen previously, and remembering where we put our glasses or keys."

Dr. Thomas Crook

A WORD ABOUT THE AUTHOR, DR. THOMAS CROOK:

Doctor Thomas Crook is a clinical psychologist. During the past six years he has served as president of PSYCHOLOGIX® Inc., an international company that seeks to detect brain disorders and find effective treatments for Age-Related Cognitive Decline, and other conditions that impair learning and memory.

He began his career at the National Institute of Mental Health (NIMH) where he spent 14 years and served as chief of the NIMH Geriatric Psychopharmacology Program. In 1985, Dr. Crook founded Memory Assessment Clinics, Inc. and was president for 10 years while it grew from a single clinic to an international organization.

Dr. Crook has been chairman of both the NIMH and American Psychological Association Task Forces for the diagnoses of Age-Related Cognitive Disorder, is a consultant to more than 50 leading international corporations, has delivered more than 300 invited lectures at major international scientific meetings, is the author of more than 200 scientific publications, and is the author or editor of nine books related to psychological assessment and treatment. He has appeared as a scientific expert in the worldwide media, including the *British Broadcasting Corporation*, European, Australian and Japanese radio and television as well as popular American television shows as *20/20, Prime Time Live, CBS This Morning, The Today Show,* and *Equal Time on CNBC.* He is frequently interviewed by the *New York Times, Washington Post, Chicago Tribune, Los Angeles Times, USA Today,* as well as *Newsweek, Forbes, Esquire, Reader's Digest* and other national publications.

After Thomas Crook left the NIMH,
he founded the Memory Assessment Clinics,
Inc. (MAC)... The MAC are the finest memory
testing facilities in the world. Dr. Crook and
his researchers led the way in refining the
earlier generation of cognition tests to make
them more relevant to real life. They pain-
stakingly developed a battery of tests that
are objective, statistically precise, yet "user-
friendly"... As simple as the MAC tests are,
they provide precise scores that help establish
the boundaries between normal but age-
related, and disease-related cognitive
performance in middle and late adulthood."

Dr. Parris Kidd

Memory Assessment Clinics Self-Evaluation Scale

Have you (or the person being evaluated) experienced any of the following problems during the past six months?

YES	NO	
☐	☐	1. Forgetting the name of a friend or family member (such as a grandchild).
☐	☐	2. Difficulty finding the right word when speaking.
☐	☐	3. Problems doing things that were once done easily (for example, balancing a checkbook, making monthly payments, preparing meals, shopping).
☐	☐	4. Becoming confused about the month or season.
☐	☐	5. Forgetting addresses and phone numbers that were familiar.
☐	☐	6. Forgetting what happened only a day or two ago.
☐	☐	7. Problem remembering what you just read or heard.
☐	☐	8. Forgetting previous conversations.
☐	☐	9. Confusing recent with past events.
☐	☐	10. Awakening during the night confused as to where you are.

Please add up the number of checks in the boxes marked "YES".

TEST SCORE: ☐

Name-Face Association Test

Instructions:

Please look at each of the faces on the next page and the name listed below each. Start at the top, and going left to right, take a few seconds to study each face and the name below it. On the next following page you will see the faces again, but in a different order, with no names. You will be asked to write the corresponding name below each face.

PLEASE TURN THE PAGE.

Name-Face Association Test

Look at the following names and faces.

Take a few seconds to study each one.

Norman

Janice

Christine

Henry

James

Phyllis

When finished studying the names and faces, please turn the page.

Name-Face Association Test

Please write the name corresponding to each face.

After writing each name, please turn the page.

_____

_____

_____

_____

_____

_____

Name-Face Association Test

The correct names are listed below. Refer to the previous test page to compare your answers. Place a check in the box next to each photo below if your answer was correct.

Christine ☐
Correct?

James ☐
Correct?

Henry ☐
Correct?

Norman ☐
Correct?

Phyllis ☐
Correct?

Janice ☐
Correct?

Please add up the number of boxes checked to calculate your score.

TEST SCORE: ☐

41

First-Last Name Test

Instructions:

Please start at the top and read each of the first and last names on the

following page. Then turn the page immediately after reading. On the

page that follows you will see each of the last names — in a different

order — and will be asked to write the first name that corresponds to

each last name.

PLEASE TURN THE PAGE.

First-Last Name Test

Please read each pair of first and last names.

Denise Jackson

Gary Robins

Margaret Taylor

Peter Johnson

After reading each pair of names,
please turn the page.

First-Last Name Test

Please write the first name that corresponds to each last name.

.... **Taylor**

.... **Jackson**

.... **Johnson**

.... **Robins**

After writing the first names please turn the page.

First-Last Name Test

Scoring:

The correct first names associated with each last name are listed below.

Refer to the previous page to compare your answers.

Check the box next to each name if your answer is correct.

__Margaret__ Taylor ☐ Correct?

__Denise__ Jackson ☐ Correct?

__Peter__ Johnson ☐ Correct?

__Gary__ Robins ☐ Correct?

Please add the boxes checked "correct" to calculate your score.

TEST SCORE: ☐

Summary

Please send a postcard with your full name and address indicating the name of each test and your scores to Memory Assessment Clinics. We will send you a report showing how your test scores compare with those of other people. We will also let you know if you are eligible for further and more detailed testing.

Please note on the postcard if you are interested in further testing or more information about Memory Assessment Clinics. All services of the clinic are provided at no cost.

SEND YOUR SCORES TO:
Memory Assessment Clinics, Inc.
7125 East Lincoln Drive
Suite A-204
Scottsdale, Arizona 85253

CHAPTER 3

SO, YOU DIDN'T DO SO WELL. DON'T WORRY.

I
f you're like most of us, you're probably a bit chagrined at your score. Don't be. Would you be embarrassed if your doctor said you had high blood pressure or high cholesterol? Likely not. Rather, you'd be glad to know. It's similar with cognitive tests that assess learning and memory functions. They only show you where improvement is possible.

PS – An amazing nutrient to improve brain function

PS is a phospholipid (a phosphorus-containing fatty acid) that is a component of every cell membrane, but is more highly concentrated in the membranes of brain cells than anywhere else. In the past, commercial quantities of this nutrient came from animal sources. Recently, sophisticated technologies have led to the development of a plant-based PS, from the source of so many healthy and useful products – the soybean.

"I've tested close to a hundred compounds for their effect on human memory, and phosphatidylserine (PS) is the most impressive one I've found so far."
Dr. Thomas Crook
Nutrition Action Healthletter, May 1997

The cell membrane, where PS is concentrated, is critical because it is a major action center in the cell: it regulates what goes in and out, how cells talk to one another and numerous other vital actions. As we age, our cell membranes become less flexible. PS increases cell membrane flexibility and it positively affects nerve cell conductivity. In the brain, PS has a profound effect on the function of neuro-transmitters, chemicals responsible for the transmission of messages from one neuron to another across a small space called a synapse. PS stimulates the production and release of specific neurotransmitters including acetylcholine, norepinephrine, serotonin, and dopamine, and helps speed the passage of messages from one cell to another. PS gives brain nerve cells renewed vigor and facilitates the formation of new neural networks.

With PS at the heart of our strategy, we can incorporate memory exercises, high quality nutrition, physical exercise, and other techniques to keep us mentally sharp well into old age.

CHAPTER 4

PS – THE EXCITING RESEARCH

"To live without a memory is to live alone." – Gilles Marcotte

REMEMBER THOSE NAMES AND FACES

Researchers at the Memory Assessment Clinics facility in Bethesda, Md., Vanderbilt University School of Medicine, Stanford University School of Medicine, and Fidia Pharmaceutical Laboratories in Italy, conducted two important studies on PS.

In 1991, we studied the effect of PS on 149 people, aged 50-75. The study was double-blind, that is neither the study investigators nor the subjects knew who was receiving PS and who was getting an inert substance (placebo). PS was given at 300 mg per day (100 mg three times per day) for twelve weeks. Subjects were assessed at the beginning of the study and at three-week intervals. Statistical analysis revealed that people treated with PS improved significantly more on a wide range of tests than did those who received the placebo, and a subset of people with greater memory impairment seemed to benefit the most. Their telephone number recall, misplaced objects recall, paragraph recall, and ability to concentrate while reading or talking all improved significantly.

"The changes are equivalent to erasing about 12 years of decline, putting a 65-year-old, for example, back to the memory status of a 53-year-old. It's important to note that the 12-year recovery in cognitive function was due to PS alone. A much greater effect can be seen when the entire program is implemented."

Dr. Thomas Crook

On one test that involved learning names of persons to whom one is introduced, subjects treated with PS went from the cognitive age of 64 (equivalent to a person 64 years old) at the beginning of the study, to a cognitive age of 52 years. They actually had a 12-year recovery in cognitive function![ix] It's important to note that the 12-year recovery in cognitive function was due to PS alone. A much greater effect can be seen when the entire program is implemented.

More Studies

In 1992, we carried out a second double-blind, 12-week study on 51 subjects diagnosed with Alzheimer's Disease (AD). Again, assessments were done every three weeks and at the conclusion of the study. At week 12, the PS subjects showed some improvement in cognitive abilities. The magnitude of the improvement was very small, however, and was seen mainly among patients with relatively mild AD. By the time patients progress to the later stages of the disorder, neither PS nor any other treatment is effective.[x]

European studies on PS show similar results. The largest and longest-running study on PS involved 425 people, aged 65-93 years, and 23 medical institutions in northern Italy. All participants had moderate to severe cognitive impairment. They were given 300 milligrams per day of PS versus placebo and were assessed at the start of the study, at three months, and at six months. The PS group improved in their social interaction and communication skills and were less withdrawn and apathetic. Significant improvement was seen in memory and learning scores in the four areas assessed: total recall, long-term storage, long-term retrieval, and consistent long-term retrieval.[xi]

Dr. Parris Kidd comments: "When this key trial is evaluated together with the other double-blind trials conducted with PS, it becomes clear that in mature adults PS can help maintain cognition, concentration, and related mental functions. Thus, particularly if accompanied by exercise and a good diet, PS may help individuals maintain mental fitness in order to meet the challenges of daily life."[xii]

In clinical trials PS was shown to positively affect mood as well and it improves scores on common depression assessment scales.

The remarkable PET scan

Positron Emission Tomography (PET) is a sophisticated, non-invasive imaging technique used to detect energy generation, particularly glucose activity, in the brain. The color PET scan on the facing page shows the brain activity of a 59-year-old female before and after taking 500 milligrams of PS daily for three weeks. Before taking PS the large dark blue region showed very little glucose metabolism. After taking PS for three weeks, the yellow-red region shows extraordinary improvement in glucose metabolism and therefore, in brain activity.[xiii]

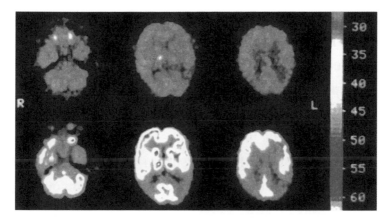

PET imaging of the brain of a 59-year-old female. The color scale indicates glucose metabolism at three brain levels, with red being most intense, and blue least intense (see color scale).
Upper images are before use; lower, after taking 500mg of PS daily for three weeks. Metabolism is increased in almost all brain regions. (From Klinkhammer 1990).

Advantages and safety of soy-based PS

PS is one of those very safe nutrients because it is already found in every cell in our body. PS can be classified as an "orthomolecule" – a phrase coined by Nobel Laureate Dr. Linus Pauling, to describe a substance that is 'orthodox' to the body, enters the body in the normal diet, poses no threat to the body's defenses, and is free of harmful side-effects.

PS has been in use in Italy and other European countries for more than twenty years and literally millions of people have taken it for long periods of time. Also, clinical studies on humans document its safety.

YEARS OF IMPROVEMENT SHOWN WITH USE OF PS FACTOR® COMPARED TO PLACEBO

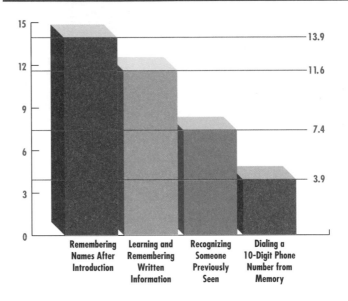

Supplemental PS is now derived from soy phospholipids, which already have a long history of use as dietary supplements and ingredients in many familiar food products. But is the soy-based PS Factor® as effective as the cattle-based PS (BC-PS) used in earlier studies?

We can unequivocally say 'YES.' In 1997 we compared the effects of soy-based PS Factor® to our previous results with cattle-based PS. The study included 50 patients who met the same criteria for ARCD as did those in the earlier BC-PS study. Subjects were treated with 300 mg of PS Factor® for 12 weeks. Their memory and learning performance was assessed at the beginning, and after three, six, nine, and twelve weeks, using a sophisticated and clinically relevant computerized neuropsychological test battery.

Notice the effects of PS Factor® on the reversal of normal, age-related memory loss in relation to various tasks of everyday life. While not miraculous, the effects are quite clear.

Most striking are the effects of PS on the ability to learn and

"A relatively large number of clinical trials have been conducted with PS. PS has emerged from this extensive clinical examination with an excellent safety record."
Dr. Parris Kidd,
Phosphatidylserine (PS): a remarkable brain cell nutrient.

remember names; here an age-related reversal approaching 14 years was observed. "That is, a 66-year-old individual performs like a 52-year-old individual after 12 weeks of PS treatment. Less striking, but still significant, improvement was observed in other tasks, some of which do not decline as clearly with age, as does the ability to learn and remember names."[xiv]

Be aware of what you buy.
Read labels carefully.

When comparing PS products read the label carefully to ensure that the label states PS potency, not just total phospholipids. To be effective, a PS product should contain appreciable amounts of PS (at least 50 to 100 milligrams per capsule or tablet). To achieve results, products with less PS require many more capsules or tablets per day, ultimately costing the consumer more.

The raw material to make PS Factor® is very expensive. If you see a bottle of PS at a very low price, ask if it is really PS Factor® that you're getting, or is it just a lecithin product containing low amounts of PS?

It is not easy to test for PS levels and very few organizations have the sophisticated technology required. Early research with lecithin was unable to accurately ascertain the amount of PS in lecithin and some products may still carry inaccurate claims of PS content based on such research. Testing can be done at some major institutions in the United States and Natural Factors Research is one of a few laboratories in North America equipped to test PS levels.

Phosphorylated serine, a dietary supplement that is also available on store shelves, does **not** work like PS. It is not a phospholipid and may cause adverse reactions.

Make sure your PS product is true to label claims, and buy only from a reputable nutritional supplement company. "The PS Factor" only works if you get enough of the real thing.

CHAPTER 5

HOW MUCH DO I TAKE?

S
upplemental PS is quickly absorbed and readily crosses the blood-brain barrier. We generally recommend 300 milligrams a day in divided doses (100 mg three times a day) for 30 days. This helps PS saturate the cell membranes, after which 100 milligrams a day should suffice as a maintenance dosage. For people in their 30s, 40s and early 50s, 100 milligrams a day is a good preventive dose of PS. If it's not possible to take 300 milligrams of PS a day to start, try 100 milligrams, although it may take longer to experience the benefits. Older people or those with significant memory loss may require up to 600 milligrams a day to start and 300 milligrams for maintenance.

Only one piece of the puzzle

Although the PS Factor® is the cornerstone of our strategy, there is more. Our approach would be incomplete if we didn't take advantage of other proven memory enhancing techniques. Just as in heart disease prevention, we do more than take effective drugs to lower blood pressure and cholesterol, we eat nutritious food and watch our fat intake. I encourage readers to make important lifestyle changes, including exercising regularly.

CHAPTER 6

GO AHEAD.
BEND YOUR MIND A LITTLE.

No matter what your age, you can prevent and correct forgetfulness. Just as you can strengthen cardiac function, you can strengthen brain function. Although it's important that you do challenge your brain, it's not critical how you do it. Memorize sports statistics, stock market quotes, Bible verses, movies, poetry or whatever interests you. Enrich your mind by taking a class, reading a serious book, or learning a language. If you're a gardener learn some of the Latin names of your plants. Just determine to challenge your brain a little more every day. Like your heart, your brain will gradually function more effectively.

Improve your memory with simple techniques.

- *Pay attention.* It takes just a few seconds to think about where you're putting down your briefcase compared to frantic searching later on.

- *Say it out loud.* When you are introduced to someone new, repeat his/her name right away and use the name once or twice afterward in conversation.

- *Be consistent.* You'll be surprised at how little you will misplace if you have one spot where you put important objects, like keys and wallets.

- *Practice remembering before you need to.* If you've got to pick up several things from the store after work, take the time to list them throughout the day. Not only will you remember your list; you will be practicing information retrieval, which can help you remember other things as well.

- *Make notes, write a list.* You're not failing if you have to write things down. Jotting down a list is an excellent memory enhancer. As the late famous psychologist B.F. Skinner used to say: "As you get older, learn to rely on memory rather than memory."

• **When you know that something must be done in the future, do as much as possible right away.** For example, if you must drop off your clothes at the dry cleaners in the morning, put the clothes by the front door, or better yet, on the front seat of the car.

CHAPTER 7

HOW TO REMEMBER JUST ABOUT EVERYTHING

In my earlier book "How to Remember Names" I offered the following specific techniques.

How to remember someone's name.

- Listen carefully to the person's name when you are introduced. Ask the person to repeat the name if you don't hear it clearly. This will rarely offend anyone and your interest will often please the other person.

- Repeat the person's name when you are introduced and once or twice afterward if you are involved in conversation.

- Look at the person and try to form a clear picture of him or her in your mind. Use the name-face association technique.

The Name-Face Association Technique: Want to remember a name?

As you are introduced, play a game in your mind by visualizing something about that person's face that relates to his name. Is there something particularly attractive, interesting or strange about this person's facial features? Locking into the person's face is the most challenging part of the name-face association process. Don't be put off by strange images that come to your mind. The stranger the image, the more your retention multiplies simply because it's out of the ordinary, or simply repeat the person's name while holding the image you have formed in your mind.

- After the initial meeting with someone, take the opportunity to write down his or her name. If you used the name-face association technique, note the distinguishing feature you used or any other information that might be helpful later.

- If you fail to recall someone's name, don't panic. The other person is probably having just as much difficulty remembering your name!

- Don't try to remember too many names at once. Decide who is important to meet and know before you attend an event or participate in a meeting.

- Go for the obvious. If you meet someone named Shirley no need to stretch to Shirley MacLaine. Think about how she does – or doesn't – look like your Aunt Shirley and you'll be ahead of the game.

- Silliness can be a great help. To remember first and last names don't wring your hands over Steven Peters. Make it Steve Pete. Amusing or even ridiculous shortcuts can be quite effective.

- Remember people in the order in which you've met them. If you walk into a conference room, start around the table – much as a waiter might – and fix each name and face into your memory, in order. It's another way to track names and faces visually.

- Sort out the names and faces as they are introduced. Don't overburden yourself with names and faces you don't really need to know. If you meet someone whom you know you'll never see or hear of again, don't bother to remember his or her name; it's just not worth it.

- If it is an uncommon name, ask about it. Many foreign names are hard to grasp the first time around, so asking about the origin of the name or even how to spell it is fair play.

How to remember everything — including where you put your glasses

- *When you misplace an object* or forget what you were after when you enter a room, mentally retrace your steps. If this doesn't work, physically retrace your steps. If you re-create the scene you'll probably remember the object.

- *Use your own voice* to reinforce your memory. Say out loud, "I am placing my camera on the black bookcase." It may seem odd to family members, but you'll improve your recall significantly.

- *When you go into a room to get something,* mentally enlarge the item and position it in an unusual spot.

For example, suppose you are going into the living room to get the latest issue of a certain magazine. As you walk from the kitchen to the living room, picture an enormous version of the magazine reclining on the couch. Most likely you will not forget what you were looking for, even if you got interrupted along the way.

- *To remember a list,* perhaps a grocery list, try the link-chain method. Here's how it works. Suppose you need the following items for your dinner: flounder, flour, tea bags, lemon, dishwasher detergent. Make the list memorable by animating it: The flounder is swimming through a bag of flour and making a mess. The fish flops onto a box of tea bags and it rains lemon juice, somewhat cleaning the fish. Then dishwasher detergent is applied for good measure. Although it seems ludicrous, this kind of technique really works.

- *To remember numbers* try the **chunking** method by clustering numbers into manageable chunks of information. A telephone number like (212) 725-4192 can be broken down into three chunks or even five chunks: (212) 7-25-41-92. Another strategy is to consciously memorize phone numbers or addresses you use frequently. Why look them up all the time?

- ***To remember what you just read,*** skim the material before you read it. Read the headings, look at the illustrations, get a sense of the material. Based on this, formulate some questions about the material you are about to read. After reading the text, highlight important sections. Now review it.

CHAPTER 8

PLAY MEMORY GAMES TO KEEP YOU MENTALLY FIT

Although it's important to challenge yourself mentally, it doesn't have to be all work and no play. Have some fun and see how your attentiveness and memory sharpen. Try two or three of the following exercises in the next few days and see if your mind begins to focus more tightly on the people, places and things around you.

- Before you sit down to read a magazine or newspaper article, prepare to summarize its contents for someone else. Be aware of how differently you approach the material. Practice finding topic sentences and make up your own headlines for different sections of the article.

- If you take the same route to work, the dry cleaners or the grocer, try to pay attention to landmarks along the routes. Pay attention to the street names as if you are going to give directions to someone later. This game will help you develop a more active sense of awareness.

- Practice creating acronyms for items on your shopping or "to do" lists. For example, pick up *dry* cleaning, drop off party *invitations*, call in *prescription* refill, and *shop* for groceries might be *DIPS*.

- The next time you are on public transportation or waiting in line, study the faces around you. Become attuned to facial features. Practice exaggerating features and studying facial composition, hair, skin, and other distinctive aspects of facial appearance.

- When you walk into a room, mentally note where ten objects in the room are placed. Once you leave the room, try to picture where each of the ten items is. Do this each day, with different objects in different rooms, until you are able to accurately recall all ten objects.

- The next time you attend a party, make a point of remembering four names. Increase that number to five, then six or more. Reinforce the names by talking to yourself several times during the event. "The woman talking to my wife is Brenda." Check your performance at the end of the event.

Help your mind with nutrients, herbs and essential fatty acids

High quality nutrition is vital to maintaining and conserving cognitive function. Neurons use more than 20 percent of all the body's energy at rest. When we are doing a challenging mental task energy consumption can go up to 60 percent. To provide that kind of energy, our brain needs to have a consistent supply of blood glucose.

Neurons are very susceptible to damage from free radicals. Excessive free radicals are often formed from smoking, alcohol abuse, environmental pollution, and chronic emotional stress. A diet rich in antioxidant nutrients, such as vitamins A, C, E, selenium and other phytochemicals found in fruits and vegetables, can help protect the brain from damaging free radicals. In addition, brain cells can be driven to exhaustion by contaminants in our foods.

The colorful carotenoids, substances that give fruits and vegetables their bright colours, also have a role to play in mental sharpness. As excellent antioxidants, particularly beta-carotene, carotenoids can slow the effects of aging. An evaluation of the dietary intake of 5,182 persons who participated in a Netherlands study, showed that a lower intake of beta-carotene was associated with impaired cognitive function. [xvii]

Ginkgo biloba extract, an antioxidant and free radical scavenger, is one herb that may protect the important fatty acids in the brain from oxidation. As one of the most frequently taken herbs in France and Germany, the extract also improves blood flow to the brain and the rest of the body.

A deficiency of B vitamins can impair our ability to think and remember. Our nervous system is particularly susceptible to thiamine (B1) deficiency. "Without it we can lose our appetite, get depressed and develop other psychological problems. With it, our energy level is up, our minds are sharp and our emotions are high. So, when it comes to the basics of nutrition, thiamine should be at the top of the list." [xviii]

Vitamin B12 is also important to protecting the nerves and a deficiency of this vitamin can cause memory loss, confusion, fatigue and a host of health problems. In fact, the B-complex vitamins work as a team, so taking a good B-complex capsule or as part of a complete multivitamin is a good idea. B-complex vitamins are not as well absorbed as we age, so it is important to have an adequate intake to maintain the health of the nerves, produce energy, and alleviate depression and anxiety.

Remember when your mother told you that fish was brain food? Well, she was right. Fish oil is high in essential fatty acids, particularly docosa-hexaenoic acid (DHA), an important building block for the brain. DHA is the major fatty acid in the gray matter of the brain and retina of the eye, comprising up to 60 percent of the fatty acids in the retina of the eye. As our body cannot make essential fatty acids, they must be supplied by the diet. There are some products available at natural food stores that combine PS with DHA.

"Buoyant health enhances memory. Your diets, stress levels, exercise and sleep habits play important roles. Specialists recommend the following tips. Eat a nutritious diet. Vitamin deficiencies – especially B-1, B-12, niacin and folate – play havoc with memory."
Retired Officer Magazine, April 1993

Exercise the body – lift those weights and start walking.

Physical exercise helps prevent heart disease, stroke and cancer, but did you know that exercise could sharpen your thinking as well? Exercise increases blood flow to the brain and helps release neurotransmitters, chemicals in the brain that are central to learning and memory. Exercise also makes you more alert, which is important for learning new things and maintaining memory. Researchers find that physically active people score higher on cognitive tests than do couch potatoes. Studies show there are significant differences in reasoning, memory, and reaction time, between those who don't exercise and those who exercise only 30 minutes a day.

Promise for athletes

In 1992, Monteleone's group in Italy reported on a double blind, placebo-controlled trial of young, healthy men subjected to exercise-induced stress. They gave PS supplements (800 mg per day) for 10 days to these young men prior to their session of bicycling to near exhaustion. PS was found to lower, by about 30 percent, the cortisol production normally associated with this form of strenuous exercise. These findings show that PS can soften the severity of the stress response in young, healthy people under stress. They are therefore consistent with the awesome capacity of PS to influence brain function at all levels of complexity. (excerpt from Phosphatidylserine - The nutrient building block that accelerates all brain functions and counters Alzheimer's by *Dr. Parris Kidd, Ph. D.*)

"When it comes to staying young, a mind-lift beats a face-lift any day." — Mary Bucella in Woman Magazine

CHAPTER 9

START TODAY TO SHARPEN YOUR MIND & IMPROVE YOUR MEMORY

W e invite everyone reading this book to check out the research on how to improve memory and learning. Then try the techniques and nutrients suggested and enjoy the results of your efforts. However, before you use the PS Factor® or any other nutrients, we encourage you to talk to your health professional. Work with your medical practitioner to develop a health regimen tailored to your specific needs. (Be aware that herbs such as ginkgo could affect other medication you may be taking. For example, ginkgo biloba has blood-thinning properties. Combined with aspirin it may cause the blood to become too thin.)

"No matter how good you think your genes were when you were born, or how bad they may have become at this stage in your life, by starting on PS and taking other positive steps you can reasonably expect your brain power will get better. You can be sure that unless you seriously move to conserve the brain capacity you now have, you will have less to work with as the years go by. The earlier you begin on PS, the better."
Dr. Parris Kidd

Developing research on how to reverse Age-Related Cognitive Decline is exciting. Take advantage of our research by implementing these strategies in your daily life. Start today to keep your brain sharp and vigorous and it will serve you well even in advanced old age.

After a few weeks of taking PS regularly and applying some of these strategies in your daily routine, you'll probably feel a bit sharper and more attentive. That's the time to test yourself again to measure your improvement. You can take the test again, or better yet, check out our website for an initial evaluation, **www.psychologix.com**.

Another website you can visit, for nutritional information and more on PS products, is that of Natural Factors Nutritional Products, **www.naturalfactors.com**.

CHAPTER 10

WHERE CAN I FIND OUT MORE?

"Those who cannot remember the past will spend a lot of time looking for their cars in mall parking lots." — Jay Trachman

We have been developing sophisticated computerized learning and memory tests for 15 years. Leading universities and international corporations throughout the United States and Europe have used these tests. Until recently, it was necessary to visit us at a Psychologix® clinic or a major university medical center, to take these memory tests. Now, we've made them available on the Internet, at **www.psychologix.com**, allowing people to test themselves in the comfort and privacy of their own home. You can have access to state-of-the-art psychological tests at no cost.

Remember that these tests have been administered to thousands of research subjects to define 'normal peformance,' and to allow us to compare your test performance with others of the same age and gender. You can compare yourself with others and take different versions of the tests after your initial evaluation, to measure changes in your abilities over time.

Most people find the tests interesting and enjoyable, not at all abstract or threatening like some tests you may have taken in the past.

Today, it's possible to prevent heart disease, slow bone loss, and improve general physical health even as we age. It is also possible to improve cognitive function whether we are 30 years old or 80 years old. Take advantage of our leading edge research to keep your learning and memory skills sharp for a lifetime.

i   Schardt, David and Stephen Schmidt. *Fear of Forgetting.* Nutrition Action Healthletter. May 1997. pg. 3-6.

ii   Crook, T.H. and West, R.L. *Name recall performance across the adult life span.* Brit, Jnl. Psych. 1990. 81: 335-349.

iii   Youngjohn, J.R., Larrabee, G.J. and Crook, T. H. *First-last names and the grocery list. Selective Reminding Test: Two computerized measures of everyday verbal learning.* Arch. Clin. Neuropsych. 1991 6:287-300.

iv   West, R. L. and Crook, T.H. *Age differences in everyday memory: Laboratory analogues of telephone number recall.* Psych. Aging. 1990. 5:520-529.

v   Youngjohn, J.R., Larrabee, G.J. and Crook, T. H. *First-last names and the grocery list. Selective Reminding Test: Two computerized measures of everyday verbal learning.* Arch. Clin. Neuropsych. 1991. 6:287-300.

vi   Crook, T.H. and G.J. Larrabee. *Changes in facial recognition memory across the adult life span.* Jnl. Gerontol. 1992. 47: 138-141.

vii   Crook, Thomas H. and Adderly, Brenda. *The Memory Cure: The safe, scientifically proven breakthrough that can slow, halt, or even reverse age-related memory loss.* 1998. Pocket Books.

viii   Kidd, Parris M. Ph.D. *Phosphatidylserine: the nutrient building block that accelerates all brain functions and counters Alzheimer's.* 1998. Keats.

ix   Crook, Thomas H. Ph.D et al. *Effects of phosphatidyl-serine in age-associated memory impairment.* Neurol. 1991. 41:644-649.

x   Crook, Thomas H. Ph.D. et al. *Effects of phosphatidyl-serine in Alzheimer's disease.* Psychopharmacol. Bull. 1992. 28: 61-66.

xi   Cenacchi, T. et al., *Cognitive decline in the elderly: a double-blind, placebo-controlled multicenter study on efficacy of phosphatidylserine administration.* Aging Clin. Exp. Res. 1993. 5:123-133.

xii   Kidd, Parris M. Ph.D. *Phosphatidylserine (PS): A Remarkable Brain Cell Nutrient.* Lucas Meyer Inc. 2nd ed. June 1997.

xiii   Klinkhammer, P. Szelies, B., Heiss, W.D. *Effect of phosphatidylserine on cerebral glucose metabolism in Alzheimer's Disease.* Cognitive Deterioration. 1990. 1: 197-201.

xiv   Katz, R.M. Goldman, R. (Eds). *Anti-Aging Medical Therapeutics,* Volume II, pp. 20-28. Health Quest Publications, Marina del Rey, Ca. 1998.

xv   Crook, Thomas. H. and Allison, Christine. *How to Remember Names: the Proven, Easy, Immediate Method for Remembering Names, Numbers, Lists... and Where You Put Your Glasses.* 1992. Harper Collins.

xvi   *How to Remember Names: the Proven, Easy, Immediate Method for Remembering Names, Numbers, Lists... and Where You Put Your Glasses.* 1992. Harper Collins.

xvii   Jama, J.W., L.J. Launer, et al. *Dietary antioxidants and cognitive function in a population-based sample of older persons.* The Rotterdam Study. Amer. Jnl. Epid. 1966. 144 (3):275-280.

xviii   Editors of Prevention Magazine. *Prevention Magazine's Complete Book of Vitamins and Minerals.* 1994. Wings Books. 2